OTHER HELEN EXLEY GIFTBOOKS
BY KATE TAYLOR
Looking for Mr Right

Published simultaneously in 2003
by Exley Publications Ltd in Great Britain,
and Exley Publications LLC in the USA.

12 11 10 8 7 6 5 4

Selection and arrangement copyright
© Helen Exley 2003
Illustrations © Kate Taylor 2003
The moral right of the author has been asserted

ISBN 1-86187-593-2

Printed in China.

Exley Publications Ltd, 16 Chalk Hill, Watford, Herts WD19 4BG, UK.
Exley Publications LLC, 185 Main Street, Spencer, MA 01562, USA.
www.helenexleygiftbooks.com

The Battle of the Sexes

A HELEN EXLEY GIFTBOOK

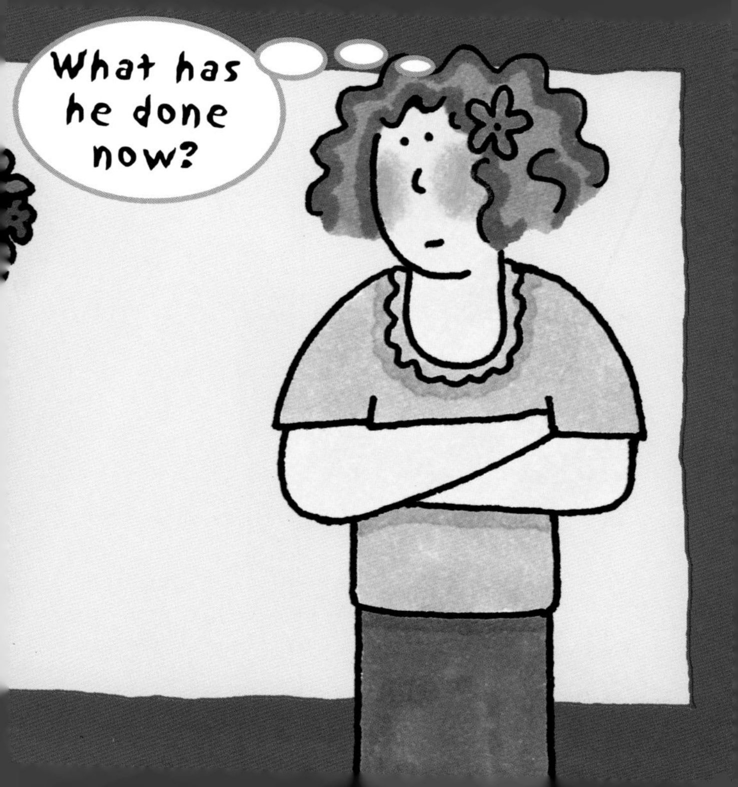
What has he done now?

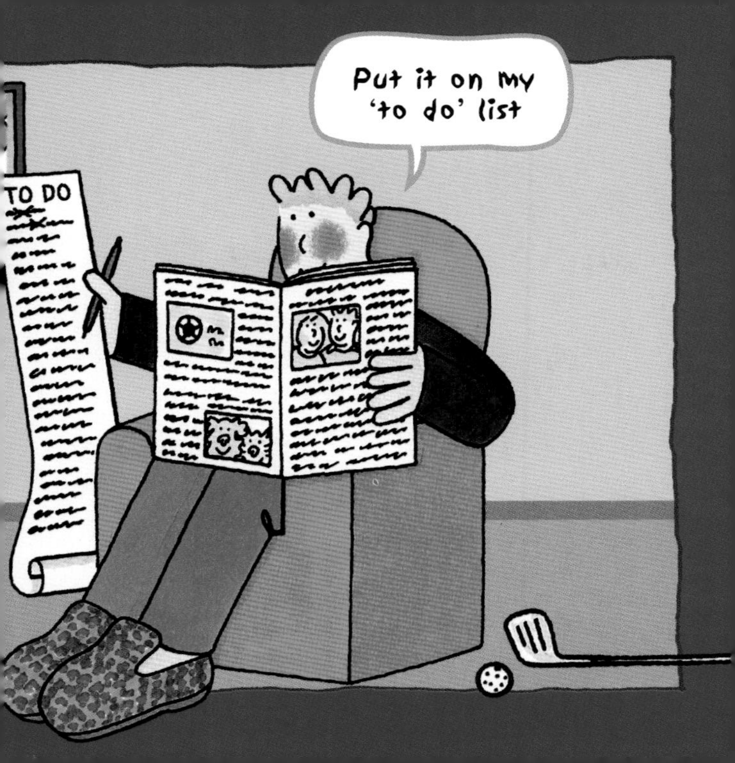
Put it on my 'to do' list
TO DO

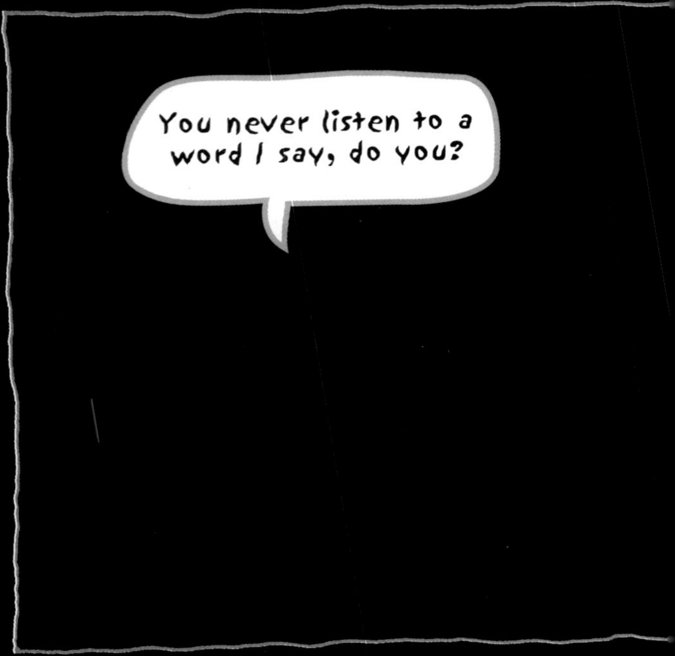
You never listen to a word I say, do you?

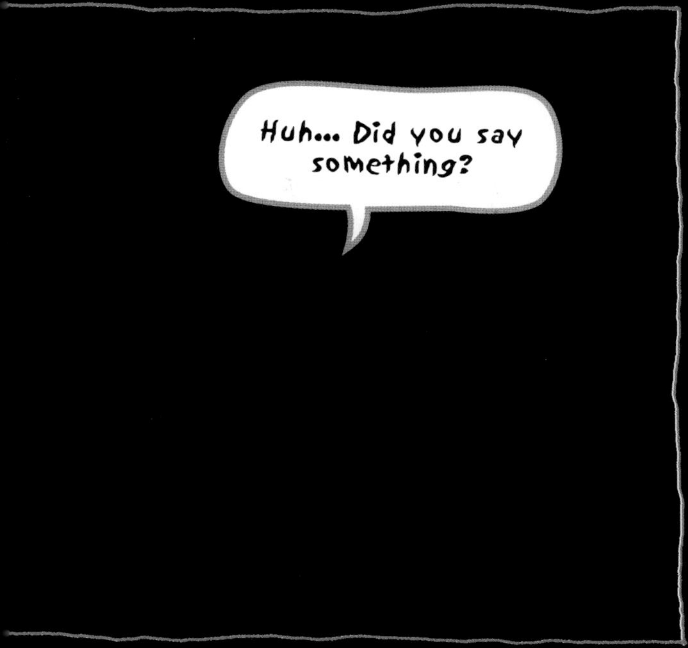
Huh... Did you say something?

ABOUT KATE TAYLOR

Kate Taylor's 42, "but maybe you could put 30 (ish)...."
She went to art college from 1979-83 and since then has worked
for an incredible number of magazines, design companies,
greetings card companies, newspapers, advertising agencies and
publishers, mainly in education and children's books.
Her animated children's series, "Christopher Crocodile" for
the BBC has sold around the world.

Kate Taylor ran her first marathon in
London during preparations for this book.
She then went on to run Edinburgh and Helsinki
while adding the last cartoons. Kate feels especially
qualified to create *The Battle of the Sexes* because,
"I have never had a smooth-running or conflict-free
relationship in my life! I have found all my
relationships with men a constant battle...."

WHAT IS A HELEN EXLEY GIFTBOOK?

No expense is spared in making each Helen Exley Giftbook as meaningful a gift as it is possible to create; good to give, good to receive. You have the result in your hands. If you have loved it – tell others! There is no power on earth like the word-of-mouth recommendation of friends.

Helen Exley Giftbooks
16 Chalk Hill, Watford, Herts WD19 4BG
185 Main Street, Spencer, MA 01562, USA
www.helenexleygiftbooks.com

Also by Kate Taylor:
Looking for Mr Right